BEHIND THE WALLS

a Chelmsford turnkey of the nineteenth century

Geoffrey Lewis

Ian Henry Publications

ISBN 0 86025 467 4

Unless otherwise noted, the photographs are by the author

Printed by Watkiss Studios, Ltd.
Holme Court, Biggleswade, Bedfordshire SG18 9ST
for
Ian Henry Publications, Ltd.
20 Park Drive, Romford, Essex RM1 4LH

`The Governor of Chelmsford Gaol'

When I was younger my mother used to say that her father had had an uncle who was a Governor of Chelmsford Gaol, but that was as far as the information went. No name was given and no period during which he was supposed to be Governor. And there the story might have rested for evermore had not my sister and I begun to research our family's history a few years ago.

We discovered that on my mother's side the family had a most interesting past, many of her forbears having been silk weavers, but they merit a separate story. As we got further with our researches I said one day that we really ought to investigate the `Governor of Chelmsford Gaol' story and find out what lay behind it.

But where to begin? Chelmsford Prison doesn't keep old records and, anyway, I couldn't give them a name. The solution came by a different route. If you go to the General Register Office, in addition to the actual records of births, marriages and deaths, they keep summary books from which you can extract, without fee, names of people, and the quarter of the particular year in which they were born, married or died, from 1837 onward.

My mother's maiden name was Parchment, a rare surname, and it has been possible to compile a chart of births, deaths and marriages over the years and where they took place. The interesting thing about this chart as you study it is that up to the end of the nineteenth century the Parchments were centred almost exclusively in Essex.

So it was that, one Sunday afternoon, I was sitting in my armchair, browsing through my copy of the chart, when I noticed an interesting sequence of names. In 1855 Sophia

Christ Church, Spitalfields. Designed by Nicholas Hawksmoor, 1725 - 1729. James married Sophia, his first wife, here, but what drew him to Spitalfields for the wedding? Is it possible that through his family's silkweaving connections he had relatives or friends here?

Parchment died in Chelmsford. In 1862 James Parchment was married in Chelmsford and in 1873 he died there. In 1896 Mary Parchment died in Chelmsford. As I looked at these entries it occurred to me that Sophia was probably James's first wife. He had married again in 1862, a rather younger woman, and thus he died in 1873, while she lived on until 1896.

If you want copies of full entries of births, marriages and deaths at the General Register Office it costs a fee for every entry, but until recently most people were baptised, and most were married, in a church, and nearly all were buried with religious rites. Thus it is possible to extract details from church registers, and many of the older registers are now kept at County Record Offices, so I have in my records copies of marriages of numerous Parchments. The next move, therefore, was to look through my list of James Parchments, of whom there are quite a number, and I found that in 1841 James Parchment, a shoemaker, married Sophia Hitchcock at Christchurch, Spitalfields, both of them shown as living at the same address in Brick Lane.

Did this mean that having married, James and his bride decided to go to Chelmsford to seek their fortune? After all, the railway from East London to Colchester, passing through Chelmsford, was completed just two years later in 1843. The answer came by studying the ten yearly census returns and very surprising it was. The 1841 census return for Chelmsford Gaol showed first the Governor, then his wife and family followed by the Deputy Governor, and then next on the list, `James Parchment, Turnkey'.

This census was compiled in March, 1841, and the marriage to Sophia was in November of that year, so James at the time was already living in Chelmsford. Why, then, had he given his address as Brick Lane and why had he described himself as a shoemaker? I have not been able to find a definitive answer to that question, so I can only surmise that he wanted the wedding to take place as far from the prison as possible and that he did not want the records to make any reference to his occupation either.

The 1851 census showed James as `Officer at the Gaol, Provisions Department', and now living at 10 Randulph Terrace, one of a row of eleven houses built in 1842 and still standing, just a couple of hundred yards from the prison on the other side of the road. Sophia's name appears under his as wife. James is shown as 60 and his wife as 64, but she was in fact nearly 71 at this time, so when they married James was 49 and his bride was 60. The marriage certificate describes them as Bachelor and Spinster, so James had certainly left matrimony until rather late in the day.

Until 1840 officers had been required to live in the prison, but then the Justices relaxed the rules and officers could live outside so long as there were always sufficient within the Gaol to deal with all eventualities. It is my guess that about this time James found himself lodgings outside the Gaol, perhaps Sophia was his landlady - who knows? - and in readiness for moving into his new house in 1842 he married her in order to regularise the basis on which they were going to live together under one roof.

Even so, having left his quest for a wife to such a late period in his life, one might well wonder how he had found time to conduct any kind of courtship when it is realised how demanding the job was. In 1841 two turnkeys had drawn the attention of the visiting magistrates to staff hours of work. They had to be in the Gaol from 6 a.m. to 7 p.m. every weekday. On Sundays they were always to be there for part of the day, and on alternate Sundays for the whole day.

In the 1861 census James, now 70, is shown as `Steward

Randulph Terrace. Would anyone looking at this row of houses realise that they are more than 150 years old? They have clearly been altered over the years and it would be interesting is an illustration of what they looked like in James's day could be found.

at the Gaol', and living with him is Mary Lapworth, housekeeper, aged 47. By 1871 James has become a 'Yeoman' and Mary is now Mary Parchment, aged 57, while James is now 79. The dictionary defines Yeoman: "A degree below gentleman, a man of small estate", and I suppose that this was precisely what James, who had retired in 1861, now was. We see from the *Chelmsford Chronicle* for 12th December, 1862, that James had married Mary at the Register Office on the fifth of the month.

The 1881 census shows Mary, now 68, as an `Annuitant' with Emily Willsher, aged 20, as `General Servant (Domestic)'; by 1891 at 78 Mary is a `Widow, Independent means' and living with her is Ada C. Sewell, `Domestic help', aged 25. In the Obituary column of the *Chelmsford Chronicle* for 28th November, 1873 is this entry: `PARCHMENT 23rd inst. at his residence, Randulph Terrace, Springfield, James Parchment, in his 82nd Year, much respected'.

Well, all this proved James's existence, and that he had a connection with the Gaol, even if it fell short of the governorship, but was he Grandfather's uncle? Fortunately, James, being a man of substance, had left a will in which there were bequests to his nephews, Samuel, William and James, and Samuel was my great-grandfather. So now the gaps were filled in: James was Grandfather's great uncle.

How though, had he come to be involved with a prison in Chelmsford when the main family occupation was silk weaving? One possible answers is that he might have been a soldier during the Napoleonic Wars. Fear of invasion by the French rose and fell and with Essex near the continent the authorities recruited a local militia, known as Fencibles, to defend the area. Is it not possible that James served with these forces and perhaps achieved non-commissioned rank?

Coronation of George IV. The celebrations in Chelmsford High Street, 19th July, 1821. *Essex Record Office*

7

The fencibles were stood down, many of them in Chelmsford, after Bonaparte's final defeat in 1815.

Who would be more likely that someone used to commanding men to be recruited as a prison officer? The possibility that he had been a soldier is reinforced by the fact that his brother, Samuel, my great-great-grandfather, was married to a woman, who came from Sligo in the north of Ireland. Fencibles could not be posted abroad, but they could be sent to any part of the United Kingdom of which all Ireland was then a part, and a large number were sent to Sligo where in 1798 there had been an uprising following the landing of some French troops. It would seem possible, then, that both brothers had been soldiers and that one or both of them were sent to Ireland, although I have been unable to discover any documentary evidence of this.

Another possible answer may lie in his description of himself at his wedding to Sophia as a `shoemaker'. This was his father's occupation and James was born in Witham and brought up in Bocking, both only a few miles from Chelmsford. At the beginning of 1820 the justices had introduced means to employ prisoners in a number of trades and it seems quite likely that James, who might well have worked in his early years at his father's trade, came into the prison initially to teach shoemaking.

Certainly, if James was running the shoemaking, he was doing it very successfully. The profits from the various activities were supposed to pay the salaries of the instructors and within a short time it is reported that all are showing a slight loss except shoe-making, which is making a small profit. Within a year the justices report a surplus of 15 dozen pairs of shoes, and it is decided to use them to supply other gaols. A few months later it is reported that not only is shoemaking the only activity showing a profit, but it is also the only one where the skills imparted are good enough to enable the prisoners on discharge to get work, and the decision is taken to discontinue all the activities except shoemaking.

The old County Gaol, Moulsham. This building stood next to the House of Correction by the Stone Bridge in Moulsham Street. This view shows it in 1810. It was demolished in 1859. *Essex Record Office*

Prison Buildings

The original prisons in Chelmsford were at Moulsham, in the centre of the town, by the bridge over the river Can. There was the County Gaol built in 1877 which housed the major criminals from all over Essex and, next to it, the House of Correction, rebuilt on this site in 1806, which was the town gaol for the more local malefactors. From a petition by James Parchment and a colleague in 1825 asking for a salary increase to be backdated we know that at this time he worked at the House of Correction.

Just before James entered the prison, the justices had begun discussions on the building of a completely new prison, as the existing buildings were inadequate for the number of prisoners held within them, and their location next to the river made them damp and unhealthy. After some discussion a site was chosen: "In a field at Springfield belonging to Lady St. John Mildmay in the occupation of Mr. Marriage situated on the South side of the Colchester Road and nearly opposite the Ordnance Depôt".

In April, 1822, six acres of land were purchased for £700, £630 of which went to Lady Mildmay and £70 to her tenant, John Marriage, to compensate him for loss of crops. The new buildings were to be constructed under the direction of the County Surveyor, Thomas Hopper; the contractors were to supply the building materials. At 12 noon on the 22nd of October, 1822, the first brick of the new Gaol was laid by Thomas Gardner Bramston, Chairman of the Justices.

The work went on for three years, some done by convicts (they were paid one shilling per week for their labour), until, on 13th September, 1825, the three surgeons of the gaol attended the new building and pronounced it fit for

11

occupation, so on 10th October the first prisoners moved in. The High Sheriff had appointed Thomas Clarkson Neale as Governor of the new Gaol on 4th September and he moved into the Keeper's house on 1st October. After a further three years, on the 14th October, 1828, the Select Committee appointed to oversee the construction of the new gaol announced its completion. On 27th December the *Times* reported: "No less than 22 prisoners have been committed to the New Gaol since the 19th instant, making a grand total now confined of 260, all of whom partook of the usual Christmas prison dinner."

By 13th January the following year, according to the *Kent and Essex Mercury*, the Justices were earnestly discussing the severe overcrowding at the new prison. One yard, for example, designed to hold 25 prisoners had 40 in it. When one looks in the same newspaper at the Gaol Calendar for the Quarter Sessions however, this is hardly a great surprise. For virtually every conviction for theft, however trivial, sentence of imprisonment follows. Two men who each stole a live fowl got respectively one month and six months hard labour. A man who stole a pig valued at eight shillings got six months hard labour and a private severe whipping. A man who stole a prayer book and sold it to a bookseller for 9d was given six months hard labour. He pleaded that the parish officers had refused him relief and he had not eaten for two days at the time of the offence, but the Chairman stated that poverty was no excuse for the commission of crime and if he had been refused relief he should have applied to the magistrates. It has to be said though that there were few alternatives; fines would have been largely ineffective as the offenders usually had no money with which to pay them.

Thomas Hopper was awarded £1,000 by the Justices for

Original main entrance to the gaol. The entrance to the prison until 1972. It is unclear whether it has been demolished or incorporated within the brickwork of the present building. Although its rather forbidding aspect must have had a chilling effect on those entering the prison, its classical style ought to have earned it the status of a listed building. Its flat roof was the scene of public executions until 1868. *Essex Record Office*

Interior view of the gaol entrance. The last view towards the outside world that convicts entering the prison would see. *Essex Record Office*

his efforts in constructing the new building and his Clerk of Works, Stephen Webb, received £50. It was not until October, 1848, though, twenty years later, that the last prisoners were finally removed to Springfield, which had been specially enlarged for the purpose. The old prisons were now sold off and the unfortunate officers who had been employed there were simply discharged. Redundancy is nothing new, but in those days there were no redundancy payments. The name of the prison was now also changed from Convict Gaol to County Gaol.

William Couthorn

When James entered the House of Correction, William Couthorn was the Keeper and a little over two years later a storm about him broke around James's head, although he does not appear to be in any way involved. There had been signs of trouble brewing as long ago as 1816 when the Justices had ordered the Governor to stop deducting one shilling in the pound from traders' bills, and all governors throughout Essex received a warning about this practice.

In 1819 a discharged debtor named Sarah Gazzard alleged that Couthorn had tried to rape her, but the Visiting Justices dismissed her claim. Later that year a letter was received from a Mr Sparrow Toms, a solicitor acting for John and Elizabeth Richardson, who had sold some of their land for the use of the House of Correction, about nuisance being caused in the use of it by Couthorn, but again the Justices upheld Couthorn.

In a special report to the 16th July, 1822, Quarter Sessions a visiting Magistrate, I. McLachlan, made a lengthy and detailed denunciation of Couthorn and comments on Couthorn's unfitness and incapacity as he keeps no accounts and one of his turnkeys, his nephew John Wood, has to do it, thus reducing by one the effective staff at the prison. He is guilty of frequent absences from duty, want of zeal, supineness, remissness and negligence.

At the beginning of 1820 the Justices had begun employing people to instruct the prisoners in making clothes and shoes. These all complained of the rudeness and lack of co-operation of the Keeper, who had often denied them admission to the prison, sometimes for several days, and the Justices had often had to rectify the position but there would be renewed complaints of rudeness often accompanied by threats of violence.

He was said to take illegal fees and there was fraud and overcharging in his accounts. He had connived at, if not actually participated in, frauds and abuses by John Wood. Mr McLachlan concluded by saying that if the Court will investigate he will provide plenty of further evidence. The Justices thereupon appointed ten of their number to look into McLachlan's charges. On hearing of this Couthorn tendered his resignation, but this was refused and he was suspended while the matter was dealt with. Meanwhile the County Gaol Keeper, Thomas Cawkwell, was asked to take on responsibility for the House of Correction and he appointed Thomas Clarkson Neale, his principal turnkey, to act as Keeper.

In September, 1822, it was advised that criminal proceedings be commenced against Couthorn, his wife, John Wood and Robert Dawson, turnkey, and the papers were sent to a barrister, Mr Andrews, to prepare proper indictments. It was also ordered that Couthorn be allowed copies of the indictment. Meanwhile Mr Cawkwell was highly praised for his efforts on the House of Correction, and it was said that Mr Neale, "Has uniformly conducted himself with a degree of intelligence, vigilance, temper and exertion which has done him the highest credit."

It was now alleged that Couthorn had induced Elizabeth Groves to swear a false oath on 13th April, 1819, to clear him of the charge by Sarah Gazzard mentioned earlier, but, as she had later withdrawn her statements, it was not felt proper to proceed with a criminal charge but a charge of 'misdemeanour' was substituted.

By September, 1823 it was decided to post notices in the *Newgate Calendar*, the *Hue & Cry* and other suitable newspapers offering £50 reward for apprehension of Couthorn and by the beginning of 1824, Couthorn, having absconded and avoided trial, was formally dismissed and Cawkwell was appointed Governor of both prisons. No mention is recorded anywhere of the recapture of Couthorn and it must be assumed that he got clean away.

On 10th March, 1823, Sarah Couthorn was sentenced and by October it was reported that she was very ill, and her doctor recommended some easing of her conditions. In January of the following year a letter was received from Sir Robert Peel, the Home Secretary, calling for a surgeon's report on Mrs Couthorn and this was provided by the prison surgeon, Dr. Gepp, and her own physician, Dr. Pritchard, but no information is available as to whether any action was afterwards taken.

The 'Workman' Story

Precisely when James moved from the old prison to the new is uncertain, but we do know that he was there in 1832 from an item in the *Kent and Essex Mercury* for 20th March that year, A man called Workman, who lived in Romford, had turned up the previous Friday in the market place in Chelmsford with a collecting box and a placard inviting donations towards a sum of £50 needed to release a friend of his called Pratt, who had been sent to prison for an aggravated assault on Parson Brooksby, who was one of the Chelmsford justices.

During the afternoon the Constable approached him and dropped one halfpenny into his box and immediately arrested him for begging. In the magistrates' court the old gentleman put up a spirited defence, pointing out again and again that he had at no time asked anyone for money, but he was nonetheless sent to the Convict Gaol for fourteen days. The newspaper took a very dim view of these proceedings having sarcastically headlined the item, "Charitable and Humane Parson and Magistrate", and the item finished, "He ... is now in the Convict Gaol, adding another victim to the law? The law of England, which, while it overlooks the gentleman beggar, who wagers a sum that he can obtain by subscription the sum of £1,000, visits the man with its full vengeance for daring to attempt the release of a man on whom the law and the church have poured the phials of their wrath!"

The old gentleman was duly released and returned to Romford, having compiled a diary of his activities during his fourteen days inside, which the *Kent and Essex Mercury* published on 3rd April. His account of the ninth day is of

The police force of Romford about 1870. The Sergeant is William Dennis, who died in 1899 after living on pension for twenty years. *Ian Wilkes*

particular interest. "Prison treatment, in common with rogues and thieves of every class, until evening, when after the other prisoners had been locked up, I was, by direction of Parchment, the turnkey, shut up some time in the hall alone and in anxious suspense, until I was ordered to the workshop and, with another, employed to saw a large piece of timber till ten at night. Bread and cheese were within my reach, and, like Tantalus, I groaned in spirit; but the reward for my sweat, which I was so ill able to lose, was half a pint of small beer, with this consolatory phrase from the mouth of the turnkey, "Now, old boy, you will sleep well after this".

Actual quoted words from James. He can hardly have envisaged when he spoke them that someone would set them down in black and white and that 160 years later a relation would be quoting them again, There may have been further repercussions of this case. The newspaper in its issue of 27th March says, "The case of Workman - It is said to be the determination of the friends of Mr. Pratt, that the committal of W. shall undergo an investigation before a higher tribunal. A professional gentleman has been consulted upon the subject and he gave it as his opinion that, unless the provisions of the Vagrant Act be greatly strained and misinterpreted, they cannot be made to meet the peculiar circumstances of the case." Whether anything came of all this, however, is not known.

Prison Escapes

Escapes were a constant hazard and a strain on both Governor and turnkeys alike. They were also frequently the cause of reprimand or disciplinary action. For example, in 1817 on 8th April eleven prisoners escaped from the old County Gaol in Moulsham and the then Governor, Thomas Cawkwell, was severely reprimanded by the Justices for, "Remissness, neglect and supineness." The prisoners had escaped by working their way through privies and into the sewers and as a result the privies were removed and 'cast iron portable utensils' supplied to the inmates: the origin of "slopping out"?

In September, 1830, William Cooper, a convicted forger, escaped. Cooper was lamplighter at the prison and was allowed the use of a ladder for his work, but under the supervision of a turnkey, and one day the turnkey, Abraham Hurrell, left him unattended for a period and Cooper used the ladder to make good his escape. Hurrell was dismissed for this, having been reprimanded by the Justices only a month or so before for drinking strong beer with a prisoner.

In April, 1837, James Dean, a turnkey, was recommended for dismissal for negligence In allowing a prisoner to escape, but he petitioned for his job back and paid £10 towards the cost of recapturing the prisoner and was reinstated. He subsequently worked his way up to Deputy Governor, but In 1853 was suspended by the Governor for being drunk on duty and when reported to the Justices he was dismissed.

While the penalties for allowing prisoners to escape were severe, there were usually worthwhile rewards when escape attempts were thwarted. For example, in 1824 a part of the old prison fell down and a conspiracy to escape was foiled by information from a prisoner called Joseph Searle, who had since been removed to the convict hulk *York* moored off Gosport and he was recommended for two years remission of his sentence.

In November of the same year an escape attempt by several prisoners was foiled by Edward Burgess, doing 18 months and William Goward, a boy of under thirteen years, who was doing two years' hard labour, and both were recommended for *six* months off their sentences.

From the point of view of this narrative, however, the most interesting foiled escape attempt is an incident that took place on 22nd August, 1837. We read in the minutes of the Chelmsford Justices that, "The conduct of three of the Officers at the prison *vizt.*; Wm Marson, James Parchment and Henry James appeared to the visiting Magistrates to merit particular approbation, they having shown great presence of mind, resolution, determination and forbearance in the discharge of a difficult duty and they were called in and received the thanks of the Visitors accordingly ".

A very full account of what happened was published in the *Chelmsford Chronicle* for Friday, 25th August, under the heading: DESPERATE ATTEMPT TO ESCAPE FROM SPRINGFIELD GAOL, and is worth quoting here in full:

On Tuesday last, during the absence of Mr. Neale, the Governor who, by permission of one of the Visiting Magistrates, had left home for South-End to meet his family, a most daring attempt was made by number of prisoners to effect their escape. Mr. N. prior to his leaving, took the precaution to visit all the cells, and made arrangements with Mr. Marson, as his deputy, for the better security of the prisoners. About five o'clock in the afternoon, C. Pigg, a turnkey, went to No. 5 yard with Mr. Fairchild,

assistant to Mr. Cremor, the surgeon of the gaol, to
see Robt. French, a convict, who represented himself
as too ill to leave his cell and go to the Dispensary.
Mr Fairchild was therefore on his way upstairs to the
cell of the patient when four convicts - Robert Coote
and William Shuttlewood (two of the three tried at
the last Assize for the murder of Lince), William
Randall, and Stephen Moss, suddenly entered the
room, seized Pigg and endeavoured to drag him into
a passage, but he clung to an iron post.

Several others then joined them, they tore his shirt to
pieces and Coote having obtained his key from him
called to the rest to follow. Coote then opened four
gates, calling to his companions, 'You b----s, we shall
all be out directly." The convicts, cheering their
leaders, followed him to the side gate leading into the
yard in front of the Governor's house, which they
supposed Pigg's key would open, but Wm. Godfrey,
a smuggler, who was stationed there, seeing them
advance towards him, ran into the turnkeys' room
and gave Marson his keys, shouting, "For God's sake
take those keys - they are breaking out."

At that moment Marson heard Pigg calling out,
"Doctor, doctor, they've got my key." The door of the
turnkeys' room was immediately bolted, and Godfrey,
armed with a brace of loaded pistols, was stationed at
an open window commanding the entrance. Marson,
having alarmed brother officers, procured a supply of
blunderbusses, swords, etc. the whole staff were
quickly armed.

By this time the fellows, to their great
disappointment, had discovered that their key would
not unlock the gate, and that Godfrey's key had not

been secured according to previous arrangement. Parchment, pointing a blunderbuss through the iron fencing at Coote, called on the party, between thirty and forty strong, to retreat or he would shoot them all; on which they all fell back to an inner passage, and, talking among themselves, appeared to be undetermined what to do.

Coote, who had sheltered himself behind a part of the buildings, defied Parchment to fire, and Shuttlewood, when he saw the muzzle of Marson's pistol, crouched down, and called out "Fire away."

A blunderbuss with a spring-bayonet was then handed to H. James, the master shoemaker, who was within the space occupied by the prisoners, and that officer immediately charged Coote who was at the time armed with a large stick. Coote retreated but made a stand at No. 5 day-room door. Parchment then came up with a blunderbuss in one hand and a pistol in the other, whilst Marson from an upstairs window levelled a blunderbuss at the party. Coote looking up called out "You b---s, run, look here," and seeing the three pieces levelled at him, called out to James, the nearest to him, "For God's sake, master, don't pull for we have done with it."

James replied, "If you've not done with it I'll soon do for you," and they were immediately driven to their cells. Marson came down, and following Coote with a pistol in his hand, pushed him into his cell, where he fell on his knees and exclaimed "Oh, for God's sake don't kill me, let me go on my knees and say my prayers before you kill me." The prisoners were all locked up and the ringleaders were afterwards put in irons. An express was sent to Southend for Mr.

Neale, who immediately returned, and made such arrangements as he thought necessary.

At the moment the prisoners got out of the yards, some of them were armed with the iron bolts, 19 inches long, which are the principal fastenings to the cells, and when driven back, a party broke to atoms the iron frame of one of the windows at the back of the prison, with these bolts, with which they would, no doubt, have killed anybody who approached them. A bolt, weighing upwards of 15 lb. was thrown out of a window, at Marson, and it fell within a foot of where he stood.

Great praise is due to the officers for their alertness, their courage, and their coolness of temper; and the prompt attendance of at least 500 of the inhabitants of Chelmsford, who surrounded the prison on the first alarm, to prevent the escape of any of the prisoners over the wall might have been of the greatest assistance. The officers who were not immediately engaged, were distributed securing other parts of the prison.

In consequence of an alteration in the law, which will take effect in October prisoners convicted of offenses for which sentence of death may now be recorded will be adjudged the particular sentence they are to undergo, and if ordered for transportation they will be immediately removed. This will tend much to prevent the recurrence of such combinations."

The ringleaders and accomplices were afterwards whipped and put in irons pending their removal to the hulks. It was ordered that the County pay Wm. Marson £20 and to James Parchment and Henry James £15 each. The references to James's evident confidence with firearms is a further indication that he may have had military training.

Shortly after this, while prisoners, maybe those involved in the escape, were being taken via Mile End Turnpike to Portsmouth, the toll collector, Edward Hitchcock, demanded toll and, on Governor Neale complaining to the Justices, he was ordered to lay a complaint and Hitchcock was convicted and fined forty-one shillings and costs. It seems that the Mile End Turnpike was linked to that at Romford, so that if a traveller from Essex had passed through Romford and paid toll he did not need to pay again at Mile End, but a prison van was surely exempt from toll altogether?

The penalties visited on prisoners for attempting to break out were invariably severe. In September, 1829, the Governor, suspecting an escape attempt, went with a turnkey armed with pistols into the garden and apprehended three prisoners under sentence of death, and they were clapped in irons. Two years later eleven prisoners were also put in irons for an escape attempt, together with two who had betrayed them because these had concealed the attempt for a time.

In 1836 after an escape attempt it was ordered that all prisoners awaiting transportation should be handcuffed until their departure. On 7th December, 1845, there was another riot by several prisoners which was put down by the Governor and officers, but, although they were complimented by the Justices, no names are given.

Chelmsford High Street, 1863. *Essex County Library*

Debtors

Imprisonment for debt was not abolished until 1869, so that throughout James's time at the prison there were debtors to look after. People who had defrauded the state of taxes or revenues, such as smugglers, were known as debtors to the Crown. By 1840 the Gaol rules forbade the employment of prisoners in most capacities and four labourers were engaged. Before then debtors had been used quite a lot as, as they were usually non-violent, they made very suitable helpers. It was a smuggler, William Godfrey, who had been instrumental in thwarting the 1837 breakout, mentioned elsewhere, by denying his keys to the rioting prisoners.

Imprisonment for debt was a useless and frustrating practice. If individuals were in prison they had no capacity for earning money to redeem their debts, but there was worse to contend with than that. Up to 1815 the Gaol Keeper got 13/4d and the turnkey 2/- for each debtor discharged. A year later the Governor was granted £60 a year to replace the fee formerly paid by the debtors.

In 1819 a petition was received from destitute debtors asking that they be excused payment of 4d a night chamber rent and asking the County to pay a shilling per week on their behalf. This request was rejected. It meant that they could not bring their own bedding into the prison and conditions were very uncomfortable.

The rules were changed a year later when it was decided that debtors should pay one shilling per week if they provided their own bedding or two shillings and fourpence if the gaoler provided it. Finally, all charges for debtors were discontinued from 1st January, 1824. In 1827 an application was made to the Commissioners of Revenue to raise Crown

Debtors' subsistence allowance from fourpence to sevenpence-halfpenny per day, but the Commissioners would only raise it to sixpence.

The last time we hear of the debtors in Springfield is in April, 1861, when they claimed the right to smoke, but the Governor considered this to be contrary to prison rules.

Children and Women in the Gaol

In these days when we have a minimum age below which children cannot be prosecuted, and when juveniles are kept in custody in specialised accommodation, it comes as something of a shock to realise at what a tender age children came under the hard regime of prison life in James Parchment's time. An illustration of the general attitude to youthful prisoners is provided in a report of the Visiting Justices in July, 1830. "The application of the principle of short periods of solitary confinement and occasional whipping, the latter particularly as applicable to boys, is likely to prove very efficacious."

In 1842, the newly appointed Chaplain, George Burton Hamilton, was even more enthusiastic about what he considered were the beneficial effects of imprisonment on the young. In his first report he says, almost lyrically, "The effect of imprisonment on these boys is not corrupting, and hardly is it to be regretted that so great a number at so early an age, are sent to prison for petty offenses ... it appears to be a salutary means of checking their evil propensities."

Before the Gaol rules finally forbade the employment of prisoners on security duties in 1840, some surprisingly young inmates exercised various supervisory functions. We read, for example, in 1838 that in enforcing the silent system, whereby prisoners were forbidden to talk together in order to prevent them from corrupting each other, a prisoner referred to only as J. S. tells the Visiting Inspector that he is a yard foreman. "I am a prisoner in Yard 3 aged 14. I have been 10 months in prison. I was sentenced for housebreaking."

In 1845, the Governor, Clarkson Neale, was responsible for administering 18 lashes with a whip to a boy of 10, who

F. SPALDING   CHELMSFORD.

Thomas Clarkson Neale, first Governor of the Springfield Gaol, who had risen through the rank from an ordinary turnkey. *Essex Record Office*

fainted afterwards, but then walked all the way home to Orsett, a distance of twenty miles. For this Neale was severely criticised by the Prison Inspectors. Perhaps the most harrowing discovery though, is that William Calcraft, the Newgate executioner, in 1831 hanged a boy of only 9 at Chelmsford for setting fire to a house.

Even so, Victorian officialdom did have occasional bouts of compassion. In January, 1856, a child named James Bennett, who stated he was 8 years of age, was committed for two months hard labour and to be once privately whipped. He received a Royal Pardon and was discharged.

Throughout the nineteenth century women were held at Chelmsford, but in the early years very few specialised facilities were provided for them. As early as 1821, however, their position was causing anxiety. In the July of that year the Justices received a letter from the Gaoler requesting the appointment of a matron for the female prisoners. This was referred to the House of Correction Committee but nothing came of it. Seven months later a woman prisoner gave birth to a child and it was established that the father was a gaoler, who was promptly dismissed, together with another guilty of assault. Even so, no matron was appointed at this time, but the wives of the Gaol keepers agreed to look after the women.

In October, 1823, Mrs Hannah and Mrs Mary Marriage offered to give Bible instruction to the female prisoners. Initially the Justices turned down their offer because, they said, the prison rules required them to provide it anyhow, but a couple of months later they did admit them, but not for very long. Perhaps the experiment did not work!

An Act of Parliament of 1823 required that women should be under the exclusive care of a matron and female turnkeys and by February, 1824, five applications had been received for the post of matron. Finally, by April three ladies had been interviewed and it was decided that each should work a probationary month and then the choice would be made. In the meantime one acting female turnkey was Mary Bearman, who was Governor Cawkwell's servant, but she had made it clear that she would soon have to give this work up owing to the state of her health.

Allowances were paid to Hester Cawkwell and Mary Neale, wives of the Gaol Keepers, for having acted as Matrons for the past two years and in July, Mrs Frances Halls was appointed Matron at £50 per annum and Sarah Clarke was appointed female turnkey at £20 per annum. A schoolmistress was also appointed at £50 per annum. No sooner had Mrs Halls been appointed than she was violently assaulted by a prisoner named Eleanor Delanty, who was prosecuted. Mrs Halls was Matron for 24 years, retiring on pension in the latter half of 1848, and finally dying in 1861 at the age of 83.

In October, 1838, it was decided to concentrate the female prisoners in the Gaol, rather than having them spread between the Gaol and the House of Correction, but even this accommodation was not entirely suitable. Ten years later, when the extension of the Springfield Gaol was complete, all the women were concentrated there. As the old buildings at Moulsham were sold off, among the redundant staff summarily discharged was Hannah Hurrell, the Under-matron.

Women were finally removed from Chelmsford around 1900, when Holloway Prison became a women's prison, but at the time some accommodation was reserved locally for remand prisoners.

The Treadmill

As at other prisons in those days the treadmill figures largely. The first mention of the possibility of introducing one appeared in June, 1813. By January, 1820, with the introduction of instruction in various trades, it was considered that some prisoners were too steeped in crime, or too truculent, to benefit from training and needed the harsher discipline of treading the wheel. However, initially the introduction of a treadwheel was deferred, pending the completion of the new Gaol. Nevertheless, a 'mill', which seems to have been different from a treadwheel, was installed late in 1820 for the hard labour of suitable prisoners.

The next year the Justices were asked to consider the introduction of a treadwheel as the mill was not working satisfactorily. Six months later it was resolved to install two treadwheels capable of employing up to 30 persons per wheel. When the treadwheel had been in use for six months it was decided that it was proving very useful. Its function was to mill flour and sometimes grist.

The sale of the flour was proving profitable, but was causing some difficulty as it was competing with local flour sellers, but the Justices were being greatly helped by Mr Joseph Marriage, who reckoned he could sell it for them in the London market.

In July, 1823, daily hours on the treadwheel were increased to nine and a half. In 1830 an improvement to treadwheel velocity in the boys' yard was reported so that three boys or two men could produce two revolutions per minute. In April, 1832, two machines were ordered for hard labour by boys, and the following year a hard labour machine for females was recommended.

Transportation

Transportation as a punishment was finally abolished in 1857, but even then the Privy Council could still order transportation and the last convicts left for Western Australia in 1863. Prisoners awaiting transportation were very much in evidence during James's years in the Gaol. Courts had the power to transport for seven or fourteen years or for life, and sentences were often imposed for what we would regard as trifling offenses.

A couple of examples from the *Kent and Essex Mercury* for 13th January, 1829, will illustrate the point. George Oakley was sentenced to seven years transportation for stealing four large sacks of barley. The account tells us that his wife screamed on hearing the sentence and was carried from the court in convulsions. William Richardson also got seven years transportation for stealing a shirt off a hedge. He had served a sentence of six months imprisonment about ten years before and the Chairman of the bench remarked that, "It was an act of justice to the public and mercy to the prisoner to send him out of the country."

Transportation was certainly a less objectionable punishment than execution, so it drew less protest. It was also a simple and final way of removing dissidents and in the early years of the nineteenth century some five thousand convicts a year went to Australia. As the century wore on though it became evident that convicts did not make such good settlers as free emigrants, and penal servitude had developed as an alternative by the 1850's.

Some particularly sad cases came into the Gaol at times. On 21st April, 1855, a prisoner was committed to Springfield accused of stealing clothing from the Maldon

Union Workhouse and, on being convicted and sentenced to fourteen days hard labour, a report was sent to the Secretary of State because in 1848 this same prisoner had been sentenced to ten years transportation, but was discharged owing to ill health. On receipt of the report by the Secretary of State, his licence was revoked and he went back to Pentonville to resume his original sentence. The unfairness of this was that on admission to a workhouse inmates' own clothes were taken away and they had to wear workhouse clothes, so that if they absconded, unless they could find a way of divesting themselves of the workhouse clothes they were automatically guilty of stealing them.

Workhouses and the prison periodically crossed each other's path. From the *Times* of 29th April, 1837: "On Monday last a spirit of insubordination manifested itself among able bodied paupers in Braintree Workhouse. About 30 men went to work as usual in the morning at the mill and continued to do so quietly until breakfast time, after which they refused to return to work unless each had ½ lb. more bread per day, and something was said about small beer. The officers were directed to prefer a complaint before the magistrate and seven men were sent to the convict gaol, Springfield, for fourteen days hard labour. The magistrates on leaving the bench room had to encounter some few symptoms of disapprobation on the part of the mob, mostly weavers."

No names are given, but, since some of James's relatives were silk weavers in Braintree, it is not entirely impossible that on this occasion he came face to face with one or more members of his own family!

The lot of prisoners awaiting transportation could sometimes be eased by the prison authorities. In January, 1828, two female prisoners came into the prison convicted of stealing from the person and sentenced to seven and fourteen years transportation respectively. A request was made to the Secretary of State that owing to ill health, they be removed to Millbank Penitentiary, and a month later this was agreed.

Springfield Executions

Undoubtedly one of the worst and most harrowing aspects of life in the prison was the execution of prisoners, in those days always carried out in public. The reforms of Sir Robert Peel in the 1820's had abolished the death penalty for a lot of less serious crimes. At the accession of George II in 1727, for example, there were fifty offenses carrying the death penalty. By 1770 this number had reached 160 and was still rising. The belief was that severity of punishment would deter offenders, but it often had the effect of deterring would-be prosecutors, since they had no wish to bring about the death of a miserable wretch for a minor theft.

However, the death penalty for capital offenses remained, and as the new gaol neared completion late in 1826, Governor Neale and the Clerk to the Justices went to inspect suitable 'drops' at Newgate and Horsemonger Lane in Bermondsey. They opted for the same style as Horsemonger Lane, which took the form of a gallows on the flat roof of the gatehouse as opposed to a scaffold in front of the building as at Newgate.

In January, 1829, it was ordered that a bell be put up for tolling at times of execution and for giving alarm when necessary. In the following year a piece of land between the prison and Sandford Lane (then known as Gaol Lane) was reserved as a burial plot for prisoners dying or being executed in gaol. From the opening of the new gaol until this time the bodies of criminals executed there had been buried in the extreme north of Springfield Churchyard, the belief being that in churchyards there was an area on the north side which was left unconsecrated for reception of the remains of those not deemed to be worthy of Christian burial. There also seemed to be rules as to when interment should be carried out. On 13th June, 1853, Thomas Hook, a prisoner awaiting transportation, hanged himself in his cell and after the inquest he was buried in the Prison burial ground, "Between 9 and 12 midnight according to statute."

The first execution at the new gaol was that of James Winter, hanged on 10th December, 1827, for the murder of Thomas Patrick, landlord of the *Yorkshire Grey* at Colchester. Although it had taken more than a year after the Governor's visit to select the most appropriate 'drop' before the first hanging, it took only eleven days to get round to the second. But executions at Springfield were not frequent enough to justify the appointment of a permanent hangman and it was customary to get the Newgate executioner to come down and perform the deed.

From April, 1829, until 1874, the Newgate hangman was William Calcraft, so he was the hangman throughout most of James Parchment's time at the Gaol. Although Calcraft was reputedly born in Great Baddow, near Chelmsford, he was the London hangman, paid a guinea a week by Newgate and a further guinea for each execution. Horsemonger Lane Gaol paid him an annual retainer of five guineas, plus a guinea for each execution there. He would charge as much as £10 for an execution outside London, but from the point of view of gaol like Springfield, that was still cheaper than retaining their own executioner.

Although Calcraft was in private life a kindly man devoted to his family, as an executioner he was a clumsy brute and his victims 'died hard'. This was because he persisted in using a short drop which was insufficient to kill quickly. It is said that his reputation for incompetence was so widespread that condemned prisoners would plead to be beheaded rather than endure his ministrations.

This grim picture emphasises the seriousness with which arson was viewed at the time. Note the six turnkeys standing there formally, with staves of office. Was James among them? *Essex Record Office*

The extreme youth of some of the hangman's victims is always a surprise in this day and age. Calcraft's hanging of a boy of 9 for firing a house in 1831 is mentioned elsewhere. In 1829, just before Calcraft's appointment, James Cook, aged 16, was hanged at Springfield for an act of arson committed at Witham. The firing of haystacks was viewed with particular severity in Essex as it bankrupted farmers and deprived agricultural labourers of their employment. In 1835 an execution for arson was witnessed by 1,200 people, most of whom were reckoned to be agricultural labourers sent by their employers as a dire warning.

Nevertheless, in 1837 acts of arson were still being done despite the awful punishment awaiting convicted offenders. The *Chelmsford Chronicle* of 20th October, in reporting an attempted act of arson at Halstead inveighed in a lengthy editorial against a series of arson attempts which it attributed to the same hand. It observed that this was the ninth act of incendiarism in the past year and that property to the value of £10,000 had been destroyed.

One of Calcraft's earlier executions was that of William Moir, a retired army officer, in August, 1830. Moir owned land at Shellhaven Creek and was angered one day by a man called William Malcolm, a fisherman, who set up nets along the waterfront of Moir's land. When Moir ordered him to remove them Malcolm became abusive and a furious row developed between the two men although, under threat, Malcolm did remove them, but Moir was convinced that Malcolm would soon resume his trespass and returned a little later with his pistols to find Malcolm again walking across his fields. There was a further abusive exchange and Moir fired, hitting Malcolm in the arm.

Considering this enough deterrent, Moir provided a doctor for Malcolm and paid for him to receive further treatment and at first Malcolm made good progress, but then unfortunately tetanus, which was nearly always fatal in those days, set in and he died within hours.

Moir was convicted of murder at Chelmsford Assizes because he had fired when Malcolm was unarmed and was offering no threat to his safety. There was a lot of sympathy for him, but a petition for clemency signed by one thousand people was rejected by the Home Secretary and he duly appeared on the fateful platform over the gatehouse. This time Calcraft must have got things right because, after a few quick convulsions, Moir died.

A double execution took place on 25th March, 1851, when Sarah Chesham and Thomas Drory were hanged. Chesham was a poisoner who had twice before been charged, but had always managed to avoid conviction. This time her luck ran out and she was sentenced, although protesting her innocence to the last. Drory had murdered a girl called Jael Denny, whom he had made pregnant, when she called on him in order to ask him to marry her. Calcraft did his usual clumsy performance; Drory took nearly five minutes to die; Chesham struggled for six or seven.

A feature of these executions which profoundly disturbed the *Times* writer who described them, was the composition and demeanour of the crowd. Estimating the number as six or seven thousand, the writer continues, "There were hardly any respectable people observable in the crowd, but a most disgusting number of women. Some of these had gay flowers in their bonnets and evidently set up for rustic belles; others were mothers giving suck to infants, whom they carried in their arms; others were elderly matrons, presiding at the head of their families, and from the elevation of the domestic spring cart pointing out to their young daughters how they could best see the execution."

43

Horrible and Bar-bari-ous Murder of Poor

JAEL DENNY,

THE ILL-FATED VICTIM OF THOMAS DROBY.

44

Charles Dickens was also a frequent critic of public executions, which he considered degrading. Only two years earlier at an execution at Horsemonger Lane Gaol, after describing in detail the behaviour of the crowd, he concluded by saying, "I have seen, habitually, some of the worst sources of general contamination and corruption in this country, and I think there are not many phases of London life that could surprise me. I am solemnly convinced that nothing that ingenuity could devise to be done in this city, In the same compass of time, could work such ruin as one public execution; and I stand astounded and appalled by the wickedness it exhibits."

There are no records which show what part James played in these executions, although with over forty years service it seems impossible to believe that he was not involved in some of them. It must have been easily the most unpleasant part of his duties, particularly as executions were carried out in public throughout his period of service. The last public execution took place on 26th May, 1863, some seven years after his retirement.

Prison Diet

In April, 1821, the Visiting Justices reported that vagrants often gave themselves up at the Gaol as the conditions, particularly during the winter, were often better than in the outside world, and in order to discourage the practice it was ruled that they would get no more beer, but would be put on a bread and water diet. Of all the references to prison catering during the early nineteenth century, this is the only one that is in any way complimentary.

In 1827, before the new Gaol was even complete, some of the prisoners confined in it petitioned for an increase in food allowance, and the Justices agreed that they should be allowed one pint of gruel and one and a half ounces of oatmeal per day after three months inside, and when this was reported to the Quarter Sessions, the Court confirmed it and ordered that vegetables should also be included to combat 'scorbutic affection' (scurvy).

In January, 1843, the Inspectors of Prisons drew attention to the prevalence of scurvy at Springfield, and recommendations were made by the Visiting Justices as to improvements in diet, heating and clothing of the prisoners, and the Court directed them to report on measures for improvement, particularly considering the abandonment of the old gaol concentrating everything at Springfield.

Letters were received from Sir James Graham, Home Secretary in Peel's administration, enclosing his Inspectors' reports and asking what the Justices proposed to do, and lengthy discussions ensued among them at their General Quarter Sessions.

Prisoners on remand could wear their own clothes and have food brought in, but once sentenced, prisoners were

Prison kitchen. Some of the equipment looks too modern to have
been there in the 1960s, but this is basically the kitchen that James
worked in during the latter part of his service. *Essex Record Office*

kept on a restricted diet until they had completed three months. For men working at the treadmill it was a hopelessly inadequate diet, The prison was also cold. Most fittings were stone and cells were unheated. Prison clothing was also considered inadequate to keep the prisoners warm. Scurvy was prevalent and the Inspectors considered it had permanently and seriously injured many prisoners' health.

One of the Inspectors, Dr. Shortt, commented on the small size of the single cells, eight feet by six and a half feet, and nine feet in height. The County Architect, Thomas Hopper, pointed out that prisoners spent far more of their time confined to their cells than had been envisaged when the prison was built and, while he agreed that the cells were too small, they would not have been if their use had been confined to sleeping.

Dr. Shortt had advocated that the prisoners should get the full diet from the date of admission In order, as he put it, "That they may be discharged not in a state of weakness, but in such a state of health and strength as will enable them at once to resume their former occupations". Mr. Tower, one of the Justices, felt that if they went too far in improving the diet, clothing and heating at the Gaol, with all the hardship that prevailed outside it would amount to a premium on the commission of crime and, "Men would commit trifling offenses to get committed, that they might be well fed, well clothed, and made comfortable."

Somewhere amid all this concern, James Parchment took over responsibility for the catering at the Gaol. In 1844, out of a list of 24 employees at Springfield, James is third, but still a turnkey and his salary of £75 per annum is the same as that of the Deputy Governor. By 1848, a new list of 31 officers allows James as Steward and Cook on twenty nine shillings per week, which is more than all the others except the Deputy Governor and Prison Engineer. James, of course, would be about 56 by this time and getting a little elderly for the more demanding tasks of a turnkey. The list includes uniform for the watchmen and warders, but James is not included, so his duties presumably no longer required him to wear it.

By 1850 a printed dietary, issued "By order of T. C. Neale", laid down daily diets for all classes of prisoner. No further record appears of complaints about food at the Gaol so it must be assumed that James was doing a satisfactory job. He kept this job until his retirement.

The Early Nineteenth Century

The Quarter Session Order Books of the Chelmsford Justices (from which much of this material has been extracted) furnish some very interesting glimpses of life in the earlier half of the nineteenth century, amongst the copious information on the prisons.

For example there are oblique references to the Mildmay Entail under which, up to 1839, much of the land on which Chelmsford stands was in the ownership of the Mildmay family of Moulsham Hall. The land on which Springfield Gaol stands was purchased, it will be remembered, from Lady Mildmay and in the earlier minutes there are periodic references to the payment of quitrent to the same Lady in respect of the Moulsham premises.

In January, 1848, a memorial was produced, signed by eighteen owners and occupiers of houses at Springfield Hill, including James Parchment, seeking permission to lead their drains into the Gaol sewer, a request which was refused. The houses were discharging their sewage into a pond in the garden of one of the signatories, and the situation was stated to be causing a serious health hazard. A usual method in this area was for newly-built houses to discharge their sewage into the nearest roadside ditch along the edge of some farmer's fields, a practice obviously much resented by the farming community. Eventually, main drainage took care of the problem, but the prison authorities were not disposed to put the Gaol's sewers at risk by allowing others to share them.

The memorial began by stating, "That in the year 1842 a Field called Lion Field in the parish of Springfield was purchased by Mr Henry Copland and being divided into parcels was absolutely sold to the present proprietors subject to a rent charge thereon." It is from this memorial that we are able to establish when James's house at Randulph Terrace was built. Incidentally, it was constructed, like many earlier Chelmsford buildings, in an off-white style of brick, known as the Mildmay brick, manufactured in those days by a local brickworks.

In September, 1831, we learn that the Shire Hall and the gaols are to be lit up for William IV's Coronation and each prisoner is to receive one shilling. Again, in April, 1838, the same is to happen for Victoria's Coronation. No entry appears in the Minutes respecting George IV's Coronation, but, in fact, the residents of Chelmsford celebrated the event in fine style with a public dinner for about two thousand people with a whole roast ox. George IV had made himself popular with the racing fraternity by reviving his mother, Queen Charlotte's, sponsorship of a race at the Chelmsford racecourse, after her death in 1818. A letter received by the Justices in 1824 shows the King to be residing then at Carlton House.

Various fees charged to debtors are mentioned elsewhere, but payment was often demanded of other prisoners, especially on entering the prison and, in 1836, the Justices tried again to stamp out this practice in amended prison rules: "No money to be taken from any prisoner on entering the prison under the name of Garnish or in any other way."

In April, 1844, four prisoners awaiting courtmartial were committed to the prison from the East India Company's depôt at Warley Barracks. After a time the Justices complained about military prisoners being committed to an already crowded civilian gaol and soldiers awaiting trial were removed to Colchester. It is interesting to note though that during the Great War the prison was used exclusively for military prisoners and prisoners of war.

The Shire Hall. Completed in 1791 to the design of John Johnson, the County Architect. This is where the meeting of the Justices, who ran the Gaol, took place.

In January, 1825, new uniforms for prisoners were agreed on and several 'slop sellers', *i..e.* clothing merchants, were approached for patterns, and an order was placed with Richard Dixon & Company of Fenchurch Street, London. In these days of continuous inflation the prices of some of the items of clothing are interesting. Jackets were 5/3 (26½p) each, a waistcoat cost 2/9 (14½p) and a pair of 'trowsers' cost 4/9 (24½p).

These days someone of the status of Prison Governor would have the use of a car. In those days a horse and carriage went with the job. In October, 1826, the Committee ruled that a chaise house and two stalled stables should be erected. The Gaol at that time also contained a mill house, a brewhouse and a bakehouse.

The Justices, in their deliberations, were always mindful of their responsibility to ratepayers for the careful use of their money. In October, 1844, it was decided that subordinate officers at the Gaol should wear uniform, and styles and design were agreed on. From the subordinate officers' point of view that was probably the good news. The bad news came nine months later when it was resolved that they would have to pay for the uniforms themselves, In October, 1847, it was recommended that police constables should not receive rewards offered for the recapture of escaped prisoners as, "Vigilance in apprehending them was part of a policeman's duty".

Every now and then the appearance of the following in the minute books reminds us that the 'Test Act', passed in the reign of Charles II to exclude Roman Catholics from holding any public office, was still in force.

"Oaths to Government.

Names of persons who produced and proved Certificates of taking the Sacrament and took the

Oaths of Allegiance, Supremacy and Abjuration and signed the Declaration against Transubstantiation at this Session,"
This would be followed by the names of some of the Justices. These entries disappear from 1828 when the Act was repealed.

Retirement

As 1861 dawned both James and Governor Neale had been in the Gaol for forty years and retirement loomed on the horizon. First to tender his resignation was Clarkson Neale and the Justices awarded him a pension of £416, which was more than his successor, Captain Henry McGorrery R. A. of the Tower, got as salary. The Committee offered him £350, which was certainly a more realistic salary for those days than Clarkson Neale's £500. He took over on 9th July, 1861, and just one week before that this appeared in the minutes:

"That James Parchment who has been in the service of the County 40 years has from age and other infirmities become incapable of performing his duty and prays to be allowed to retire and the Visiting Magistrates recommend that the Court will please to allow him to give notice in compliance with the *5 &6 Vic C 98* that it is his intention at the next Quarter Session to apply for such superannuation allowance as the Court may think fit to grant".

On the 15th October appears, "James Parchment having been in the service of the prison for upwards of 40 years granted 10/12ths of his salary of 29/- as pension viz. £1-4-2 per week." John Rayner, Assistant Cook, was appointed Cook and Steward in his place.

Thus James ended his service never apparently having blotted his copy book. It would have been easier in some ways to compile details of his career if he had, since it would have occasioned a few more references to him. Prison officers appear on the record all the time on disciplinary charges of one sort and another and are warned, reprimanded, fined and quite frequently dismissed. Even at the beginning of 1861 we read that Richard Clark, the Head

Turnkey with 31 years service, who had had his salary reduced in 1857 from £65 to £55 per annum for misconduct was to go up to £60, so that even then he was receiving less in salary than James got as pension. Clark, in fact, retired a few months later himself.

Even Clarkson Neale had not managed an entirely unblemished career. In July, 1844, Ebenezer Clark, a warder, was suspended for a period for keeping a beer shop, and the miller and the baker in the Prison were both referred to the Visiting Justices for the same offence and they recommended to the Court of Quarter Sessions that no officer in the employ of the Prison be allowed to have any other occupation or employment. Clark was suspended by Captain Skinner, one of the Visiting Justices, and on 2nd July T. C. Neale was severely reprimanded by the Court for using the expression "Captain Skinner is a blackguard." Neale was first called in and reprimanded by the Visiting Justices after tendering a full apology, but a very detailed report in the *Chelmsford Chronicle* for 5th July relates how Captain Skinner had raised the matter again at the full Quarter Sessions. The report takes up four feet and three inches of column space in a closely printed broad sheet newspaper. The matter was settled but not before the gallant Captain had made an extremely lengthy and bitter complaint.

We have no record of how James spent his retirement other than that he married Mary on 5th December, 1862, Just ten days before Clarkson Neale had died, so although the two, having worked together for so long, were probably good friends, he obviously didn't spend his time in Neale's company. The next information we get on James is from his will, which was proved on 26th March, 1874. This is a three page document with bequests totalling an estimated £3,000, a considerable sum for those days. It speaks of real estate,

Ebenezer Strict Baptist Chapel, where Mary, James's second wife, was a devout member. It was built in 1802 and was part of a more intimate street scene until the Parkway was cut through in 1970, leaving it on an exposed corner with heavy traffic roaring past.

copyhold estate and shares. He leaves an income to his wife and his three nephews, all to be financed out of the income from his properties.

Under the report for 6.1.1874 appears, "Pensioner John (*sic*) Parchment died on the 23rd November." Mary therefore lived on in comfortable retirement, with a maid in residence, until the end of 1895. During her latter years she was a staunch supporter of the Ebenezer Baptist Chapel in New London Road to which she left some bequests and in a record book still kept at the Church there appears in the most elegant copper plate handwriting this entry dated 23rd February, 1896, "The death of Sister Mary Parchment was reported to the Church, and it was also stated that she had by her will left a legacy of £20 to the Church, and also a further £5 to the Sunday School."

And so the story ends. There are many gaps in it which I could fill by surmising what happened, but I am not keen on doing that. There are, as always with a story of this sort, a number of `If only's'. If only James had kept a diary and I had possession of it. If only my mother and grandfather had been able to see all this material, what might they have been able to add to it from stories handed down? And above all if only a photograph of James were available, that alone would be worth a lot.

One must not grumble though. Considering how long ago the events recounted here took place, it is fortunate that so much has been extracted.

INDEX